Two Sides to Every Story

A Short Guide to Cross Cultural Awareness in Papua New Guinea

Philip Fitzpatrick

Contents

Preface

I first went to Papua New Guinea as a patrol officer, or *kiap*, in 1967 and then worked as a project officer on an enquiry looking at land tenure systems. Following self-government I returned to Australia and worked for the South Australian government in Aboriginal heritage for twenty years before setting myself up as an independent consultant. I returned to Papua New Guinea in 1997, working in mineral and oil and gas exploration, firstly as a camp manager and then later as a social mapping consultant.

In all that time I have had the opportunity to observe interaction between indigenous people and Europeans. In Papua New Guinea this involved expatriates coming into the country on short term consultancies and work contracts. Also, as part of social mapping studies, I have rendered advice on how I thought interactions between various companies and particular local Papua New Guinean communities should be handled. On occasions I have also delivered talks, seminars and workshops on the same theme.

For what it is worth, this short book summarises some of the general conclusions I have arrived at through this experience and some of the reasons why things happen in the cross-cultural context, and what might be done to mitigate the less desirable aspects.

That said, I should also point out that the take-up of my advice has often been perfunctory; companies and company management in Papua New Guinea generally work to timetables that do not allow the luxury of getting things right rather than getting things done. On most of the projects on which I have worked expediency has tended to trump good relationships.

At the individual level I also realised that you can conduct as many cross-cultural workshops as you like but you can seldom influence people to modify or change their ingrained habits, behaviours, prejudices or attitudes. This sort of change takes time and experience and this is generally in short supply in the corporate world.

In that vein, the best I can offer is to say this is what I think and this is the way I think you should behave, how you do that, however, is up to you. Get it right in the beginning, establish the relationships and respect you need, and you'll save yourself a lot of angst, and probably money, in the long run.

Unfortunately, I have often been in the position of saying, 'I told you so', and while taking some satisfaction from this I often rue the pig-headedness and conservatism that led to it. But, then again, what do I know? The exigencies of business often escape me, I'm just a simple writer and sometime consultant, not a businessman.

Introduction

Culture is an extremely difficult thing to define because it encompasses an extremely wide range of human behaviour. To attempt to enumerate all of these aspects is probably not worthwhile.

This small book is primarily concerned with the interactions between Papua New Guineans and expatriates of European origin, mainly Australians and Americans. Of late there have been many workers entering Papua New Guinea from China and other parts of Asia. These people seem to be quite different to the current and long term Asian workers and populations in the country. There are indications that the relationships between these 'new' Chinese and Papua New Guineans has its own set of problems and requires broader study. This is beyond the scope of the present discussion.

People like anthropologists and sociologists have been systematically recording and analysing cultures for many years now and, in many cases, still fail to agree over their interpretations.

Although they claim to be objective in their work it is evident that most of them use their own cultures as the benchmark for their analysis. This can skew any interpretation dramatically.

There are well over 700 distinctive languages in Papua New Guinea. The largest language groups comprise several hundred thousand people but there are also language groups of less than 100 individuals who speak their own distinctive language. Added to this are countless thousands of dialects. This makes for an extremely diverse cultural mix.

What may be custom in one area is not necessarily the custom in another area. Even language groups living in close proximity to each other may have different and even opposite customs. For this reason it is important not to generalise too much when discussing cultural matters. Just because one group follows a particular custom doesn't mean that everyone else in Papua New Guinea follows the same custom.

This fact must be borne in mind when reading this book. The following is an attempt to pick up some of the more common cultural themes without being unnecessarily prescriptive. Even these themes may vary from place to place and they should be interpreted more as an introduction to general principles than as a definitive guide. There is no substitute for local knowledge and this should always be sought when dealing with cultural matters.

The best people to analyse a culture are probably the people actually living in the culture. Failing that, living within a different culture for some time will probably provide the best appreciation of it. Reading or being taught about a culture is a good start because it can alert one to the things to watch out for and can soften the impact of the "shock of the new".

When two cultures come together, as when expatriates meet Papua New Guineans and vice versa, those aspects which seem to come to the fore are the differences rather than the similarities. These differences can be very profound or quite subtle. The impact upon the individuals involved can also be quite profound.

One of these impacts is known as '**cultural shock**' and it occurs on both sides of the fence. Culture shock is essentially the feeling of being overwhelmed by something new and strange and beyond a one's normal and previous experience. The effect disappears with time as the opposing cultures get to know and feel comfortable with each other.

Culture shock is a type of stress which may include disorientation, depression, apathy and irrational or inappropriate responses. One of the overwhelming urges that it generates is the need to leave the environment responsible for the stress and go back to one that is more familiar. This is normal. Once this initial period is over most people react in a very positive way and find that they are enjoying the experience of the new culture and learning about it.

Culture shock can happen to an expatriate coming straight from his or her home in, say, Houston Texas, as much as it can happen to a villager coming out of a traditional setting and into an industrial workplace such as a drilling rig. It is very important that people be given time to adjust to their new situation. This is a time when many mistakes and misunderstandings can occur.

For this reason it is important to be well prepared and to have an open mind when entering a new culture. Reading and taking courses about the culture is a good way to become prepared.

It is also important to be aware of one's own inbuilt prejudices and to be prepared to reflect on them in an objective manner. These prejudices are generally the product of one's upbringing and the social environment in which it occurs. Some prejudices, such as racism and sexism, will work against acceptance of the new culture and will ultimately diminish the experience of it. Sometimes people are unaware that they hold these sorts of prejudices and will be surprised when they surface in the new environment.

Other prejudices, such as those related to simple things like food preparation or personal hygiene, are less obvious but can still impact negatively upon one's experience of a new culture. In other words, part of the process of learning about a new culture involves analysis of one's own culture and self.

A good habit to develop and which can assist in softening the blow of culture shock is the habit of self-reflection. Most of the time we actually self-reflect without realising it. Self-reflection is simply asking yourself 'what happened?' What could I have done to improve the situation? And how can I approach the issue next time?

It is not necessary to carry out such analysis all

the time but simply to be aware and open to the process, especially if you encounter particular situations which you find confronting, different, or even hostile. Such analysis can have very positive effects so that when someone returns to their own culture they will find that they have experienced a kind of personal enlightenment which their relatives, friends and colleagues may not understand. Viewed in these terms exposure to another culture can be a very worthwhile experience.

Some companies try to protect their expatriate staff by limiting their exposure to the people in the area where they will work. Part of this strategy has to do with concerns about **security** but in the long run it tends to be counterproductive and doesn't help people understand each other.

An expatriate whisked from the airport to a secure compound will develop a sense of siege where what is outside the compound fence is a threat to him and he will carry this feeling forward with him and it will affect his work and dealings with local employees for a very long time.

A better scenario is to make people aware of their new environment and to instil in them a healthy sense of where to be careful and where to be more open.

A similar thing can happen to Papua New Guineans when they enter a secure and confined work place. Having come from an egalitarian environment where everyone interacts all day long and everyone knows each other's business, entering an industrial complex with its rigid rules of behaviour can severely inhibit their approach, attitudes and regard for their fellow expatriate workers.

While it is not expected that the attitudes of either expatriates or Papua New Guineans, which have both been developed over many hundreds of years, can be modified overnight it helps if they start off with at least a small understanding of each other's cultures.

As noted above, these cultures are both extremely complex and can never be understood in their entirety. Rather, by concentrating on some of the main **differences** it might be possible to soften the impact of such things as culture shock and prepare the way for a degree of understanding on both sides.

In doing this a first significant point needs to be understood. This is that neither culture is **superior** to the other. They have simply evolved in different ways. While one culture adopted an Industrial approach to life the other has opted for an Arcadian approach.

In many respects these approaches have been dictated by their different environments but in the final analysis both expatriates and Papua New Guineans are all human beings under the same sun. They all experience the joys and sadness of life and they are all prone to the less attractive aspects of humanity, such as greed, jealousy and cruelty.

One should also not make the mistake of assuming that everyone automatically understands your culture because you are English, American or Australian and your culture has been spread far and wide over the world. Neither should you assume that everyone regards your culture as superior. In many parts of the world western culture is viewed as degenerative and even evil. Sometimes these criticisms carry weight.

People may know about your culture but often that **knowledge is superficial** and has been picked up from artificial and unreliable sources like television programs and movies. While they might know what your culture looks like they do not necessarily understand why you do certain things in a particular way or believe in the values that you do.

For many people what you do and say can be as puzzling and inexplicable as what you see them do and say. In other words, **cultural differences cut both ways**.

It is also important to remember that what might be the cultural norm in one place in Papua New Guinea may not be the norm in another, even if they are in close proximity. Extrapolating from what you understand about one group can be misleading and sometimes dangerous. This is particularly so when contrasting coastal and highland communities.

Cultural 'rules' are also never 100% accurate. There are always variations and subtleties. Being categorically about a particular custom can often lead to misunderstandings and the possibility of denying people's rights.

For instance, saying that men inherit rights to land or other valuables through their fathers in a particular area might not be entirely true. Most men may do so but there are always exceptions. Someone adopted into a group from outside may also have legitimate rights to land and it may be that someone might decide to pass on their land to someone outside their immediate family. One has to be very circumspect when dealing with custom and culture.

History has proved that nations based on an industrial model eventually steamroll over those with a rural emphasis. This is happening in Papua New Guinea just as much as it is happening in rural areas in Australia and America. In the latter places the people have some idea about what is rolling over them but in Papua New Guinea it is still all relatively new and confusing for many people, especially those living outside the cities as subsistence farmers or as hunters and gatherers.

Papua New Guinea and its people are going through an incredibly difficult period of adjustment, one which will occupy them for generations to come. Social and technological changes which most of the world experienced over a period of two to three thousand years have overrun their society in a single century.

The degree to which people in Papua New Guinea have coped with this change is quite variable. For those in rural areas with little education the changes have been very difficult and they have had trouble keeping up with it.

More educated people have taken it in their stride remarkably well. Many of the changes are related to new digital technologies which deal with information and knowledge and the speed and way in which they are processed. Knowledge has always been widely valued in Papua New Guinea and is a significant attribute of traditional leaders so the ready adaption of new forms like the internet and mobile technology is not really surprising.

Not only have educated people taken to this technology well but so have large sectors of the less educated. Social media has had a profound effect upon Papua New Guinea in the last few years and is changing the way that business and politics are conducted very rapidly.

In remote parts of Papua New Guinea, far from the coast, stone tools were still in every-day use sixty years ago. And yet in far-away Dubai, the award-winning airline, Emirates, employs several Papua New Guinean First Officers and Captains, men who trained and gained experience with Papua New Guinean airlines. This incredible **rate of change**; stone-age to space-age in three generations, cannot be endured without stress and strain.

The huge, world-wide upheavals of the eighteenth and nineteenth centuries encompassing industrialization, the move away from artisanal modes of manufacture and frequently brutal reforms in land ownership and rural production, which led to the wealthy first world, passed Papua New Guinea by. All along, though, Melanesian customs, lifestyle, logic and ethics remained as an ethos existing in a successful, if isolated, independence from the rest of the world.

It is a mistake to assume that the more educated a person is in Papua New Guinea the less they know about and conform to traditional customs. This is particularly so in the case of sorcery and magic. Even though educated people will deny believing in these things at base many of these beliefs still lie just below the surface. Most educated people still follow traditional marriage customs and pay bride price and enter into betrothals. Educated people even engage in old customs like polygamy.

In the end, good relationships between two different cultures relies heavily on the ability of both to sit back and think, to be reflective and open to new ideas. Crucial to this is communication. In so many cases a failure to communicate, discuss and accommodate new ideas and norms is at the crux of inter-cultural conflict. Instead of just wondering why a person has done something you should take a step further and ask them. A simple question like, 'Why have you done that?' can be the gateway to success.

From the Expatriate Perspective

The traditional social unit in most of Papua New Guinea is the **clan**. Clans generally have a common ancestor, usually a male. Clans are comprised of extended families. Sometimes clans are divided into sub-clans. A collection of clans with a common language are sometimes described as 'tribes'.

As clans get bigger and bigger with more members they sometimes split and new clans are created. Conversely, some clans shrink and eventually become extinct.

Each clan usually has a **'headman' or 'chief'**. These men are not absolute rulers. There is generally no hierarchy of leadership and formality is loose. Traditional leaders acquire their positions through personal attributes, charisma and acumen; that is, they are self-made leaders.

They tend to lead in matters related to ritual, sorcery and inter-clan matters and have a detailed knowledge of their clan's history and customs. Most clan decision making is reached by **consensus** with everyone involved. The leaders tend to lead and co-ordinate discussions but do not have a form of veto.

Traditional leaders tend not to be at the forefront of modern day economic and social matters, although they may have significant roles in the background. The tendency nowadays is to put forward younger, educated men in negotiations. This is an important piece of information for expatriates to remember, especially as most expatriates come from western style educational institutions and workplaces which operate using western style management systems.

The expected transformational or transactional

leadership styles which an expatriate may expect are not the norm in Papua New Guinea; instead alternate and less understood leadership styles such as the paternal leadership style are more evident. It could be argued that the term 'leadership' may in fact be wrong for use in Papua New Guinea, where instead 'influence' plays such an important part in Papua New Guinea culture and helps in understanding the importance of relationships to people.

While these younger men might exhibit an outward deference to their elders they increasingly pursue more **limited and personal interests**. This has resulted in a situation where there can be multiple and occasionally contradictory voices purporting to represent the clan.

These voices may include men living outside the clan area who have gone away to work and men who hold leadership roles in non-traditional areas such as government and private enterprise. Increasingly, people who have acquired wealth, sometimes in significant amounts and often through dubious means, put themselves forward as leaders. Sometimes these claims are tenuous and exist within a system of constantly changeable patronage.

Women exert less power in the traditional sense but should not be discounted because they are often active in the background. Younger, educated women are slowly making headway in an otherwise male dominated sphere.

Clan loyalty is very strong. Membership of a clan involves an intricate web of obligations that binds people together as a supportive whole. An individual knows that if they get into difficulties they can fall back on the resources of the clan for help. They also know that if a member of their clan needs help they are obliged to assist, be it through assistance to clear a new garden site, build a new house or provide money to buy food.

Traditional Papua New Guinean economies are based on exchange and compensation. Every time someone gives another person something there is an expectation of reciprocity. When a Papua New Guinean receives a gift or favour they know that at some time in the future it will have to be paid back.

Prestige and power are derived from the amount of valuables, like pigs or money, which has been given away. A wealthy man in traditional Papua New Guinean society is one who has given much away. A 'bigman' in Papua New Guinea society, especially in the highlands, is someone who has accumulated great wealth and then given much of it away. This has been translated into the modern age where many politicians see themselves as latter day 'bigmen'. These modern 'bigmen' differ markedly from their forbears in that self-interest lies at the core of their relationships, not the wellbeing of the clan or tribe.

It is also common for individuals to use their largesse to create obligations and exercise power over the individuals to whom they have given things. Favours are not given for nothing. By supplying a woman as a bride there is an expectation of payment in the form of a bride price or another woman suitable for marriage to a relative for instance.

Using the same logic allowing a mining company to extract minerals from clan land involves a perceived obligation for payment or compensation regardless of the fact that minerals are owned by the state. Using clan land to erect an exploration camp implies the same sort of obligation.

Whereas favours have a palpable value, so do disfavours. A disfavour, such as an injury or murder of another person carries a price which is defined in terms of compensation owed.

An expatriate who innocently makes a gift to someone should be aware that in the mind of the person receiving the gift an obligation of reciprocity has been created and there has been a subtle power play at work.

During any negotiations undertaken with Papua New Guineans, be they individuals or clan groups, the reciprocity element should always be borne in mind. For every concession won by either side there will always be an expectation of a corresponding price.

Internecine **clan warfare** has been going on for thousands of years and it still persists today, albeit sometimes in a toned down and more subtle way. In many parts of the country, especially the highlands, conflict is still the natural state of affairs.

In many of Papua New Guinea's societies the cult of the warrior is still extremely pervasive. Young men are still trained in the nuances of war, including the pragmatic aspects of killing and the magical ethos in which much of it takes place.

Violence has always been essential for the preservation of clan lands and clan reputations. An eye for an eye and a tooth for a tooth is a belief inculcated into young men and perpetuated as they progress through manhood to the higher echelons occupied by respected elders. To a Papua New Guinean warrior the pain and suffering that he might inflict on people outside his clan is immaterial to the greater cause of clan solidarity.

Tribal and inter-clan **warfare** is still a fact of life in many parts of Papua New Guinea. In some areas like the highlands the principle of **revenge and payback** is an integral part of those wars. In the absence of suitable compensation for a death in war another death on the opposing side is generally required. That death doesn't necessarily have to be of someone engaged in the original conflict.

Because the clans operate as inclusive and homogeneous bodies they share a collective responsibility in the payback system. That is, everyone in the clan shares both the glory and blame for the death of a warrior in the opposing clan and are a potential target for a revenge attack. Very often the individual who struck the mortal blow is not the victim of the revenge attack. If they are unreachable the revenging warriors on the other side will often take a substitute instead. This could be an innocent woman or child from the opposing clan who happens to be easily accessible.

It could also be an innocent person from the offending clan on a company worksite who had absolutely nothing to do with the war and the killing. When a tribal or clan war erupts and people are killed everyone in the clans involved are potential targets and live in fear of being ambushed. In a workplace, such as a mine site, there are likely to be local workers from all the clans involved and they will become very nervous and suspicious of each other. When this happens it is important for the company to know which clans are involved and which of their workers belong to the respective clans involved so that **avoidance strategies**, such as closing the worksite down, can be quickly put into place. While there is never really any danger for expatriates during times of warfare their Papua New Guinean staff or co-workers may be in real peril.

In areas where clans are still engaged in simple subsistence farming its members are very much concerned to retain land. With increasing population pressures they are also keen to expand their borders as much as possible. In these places land is still being acquired by conquest and compensation. Anything that impinges on this process, like a large resource development, is first and foremost considered a threat. It is as if another clan from over the hill has come down looking for a fight and the spoils that go with it. And in Papua New Guinea when rights and entitlements look like being threatened the natural response is aggression. Sometimes this aggression is immediate and illogical.

Communities in Papua New Guinea are mostly small and insular. Beyond the immediate community everyone is a potential enemy. Those potential enemies may be several kilometres away or they may be just over the next hill. The sense of a larger **community spirit** that you might see in countries like Australia and America is hard to find in Papua New Guinea. When you go into rural Papua New Guinea you are, to all intents and purposes, entering a potential conflict zone.

This is something that many people like resource developers don't seem to appreciate. When it comes to land your **simple subsistence farmer is no pushover**. They can become extremely difficult people to deal with and they are prepared to trample over other people's rights to protect their patch and get what they want. To steal from another clan or trick them out of something that is legitimately theirs is a coup, not a crime. This includes getting a first foot in the door when it comes to possible benefits from a resource project.

Clan warfare can be the end product of **failed mediation** when all other avenues for resolution have been exhausted. There is a very effective **village court** system in Papua New Guinea which deals with civic and minor criminal matters as well as **provincial land courts** which deal with matters related to land disputes.

In the first instance villagers will attempt to resolve disputes themselves using village elders or local 'bigmen' as **mediators**. If this fails a village court magistrate may be called in to settle the dispute. While these are legally constituted courts with enforceable and binding verdicts they are conducted in an informal way, often in the village setting. Village courts also operate in urban areas, including the settlements around big towns.

When a resource developer goes into a new

area their activities may lead to the revival of old, even **ancient, unresolved disputes**, particularly in relation to land and boundaries. Most villagers can usually sort these things out themselves and it is just a matter of giving them time to do so. It is important to stand back and not get involved in this process, even if it is tempting to do so and the various protagonists lobby you or seek your support. Rushing the process because of your own **deadlines** can often exacerbate rather that mitigate a dispute.

If the villagers can't resolve a problem they should be encouraged to call in a village court magistrate or the provincial land court assessor. It just needs to be borne in mind that these people are generally overloaded with work and lack crucial resources like transport. There is nothing wrong with **assisting them** to visit an area but involvement in the actual dispute should be avoided at all costs.

Papua New Guinea has an **annual growth rate** of about 3%, which is extremely high. Some 40% of the population is under 15 years of age. In a country where subsistence farming is the major activity of some 75-80% of the population this rapid rate of expansion is creating real pressure on land, particularly in the densely populated highlands. Land tenure in these areas has often had a history of conquest and invasion. In a warrior society invasion and conquest is viewed as a legitimate way to alleviate **land pressure** and this belief still pervades.

At a more general level membership of a clan implies the **sharing of its resources** in various ways. Old people no longer able to tend their gardens must be provided with food and other assistance. Orphaned children are cared for by the clan, as are widowed women.

The emphasis on social networks in Papua New Guinean society contrasts markedly with the emphasis on the individual in modern western societies. In the west individuals are encouraged to strive to advance themselves both economically and socially, often at the expense of others. In western transactions, both social and economic, individuals seek to maximise status and profit with little regard for those upon whom losses are inflicted.

The training for this role begins in childhood where games are conducted in terms of winning and losing. In traditional Papua New Guinean societies childhood play is more about cooperation. Papua New Guinean children exposed to the games of western children have difficulty in adjusting to inherently selfish individual behaviour. They feel acutely embarrassed when asked to play competitive games solely in order to win.

This also transfers to other levels in school where they temper the need to excel by avoiding situations where they are seen to be gaining advantages over their classmates. This attitude carries on into adulthood and explains why Papua New Guinean workers are often extremely uncomfortable with individualistic and overly aggressive and ambitious expatriates.

This web of inter-related dependence is generally referred to as the **'wantok'** (one-talk) system. As people have become more mobile and have ventured out beyond the traditional realms of the clan the system has gone along with them and evolved to include members of language groups.

Dedication to the *wantok* system pervades all activities in Papua New Guinea and exists from the highest office in the land right down to the most insignificant individual in the village.

One of the areas where the most detrimental effects of the system are felt is in the political sphere. The party system in Papua New Guinea did not evolve into a situation where there are two strong parties representing the right or left or even a government and an opposition. Neither did a strong core of independents evolve or minor parties with particular biases such as a "green" agenda. Instead there exists a multitude of different parties with very little ideology but many disparate, narrow and varied vested interests.

During elections there are typically dozens of candidates for each electorate, usually representing very small 'tribal' areas. A considerable amount of vote buying occurs during elections and violence is not uncommon. In the Papua New Guinean voting system a winning candidate may only need to garner a small percentage of the overall votes cast.

It is only after the elections that the wheeling and dealing occurs and winning candidates coalesce into 'parties' and coalitions until one is big enough to form government. Bribes and payoffs feature prominently in these negotiations with candidates often taking the best offers regardless of political positions or policies.

Once installed, government ministers will begin filling key posts with *wantoks*. In most terms of government the districts from which the prime minister and his senior ministers come from provide most of the key public service positions. Senior public servants, especially those in key positions such as the police and military, do not enjoy secure tenure by any means because of the *wantok* system. The system places loyalty above qualifications and suitability for a job and inevitably results in massive inefficiencies.

The system can also make the situation of the incumbent government precarious and often results in much crossing of the floor in parliament and motions of no confidence.

Overall the *wantok* system makes the business of government in Papua New Guinea very uncertain and fractious.

Like many traditional customs in PNG the *wantok* system has been **subverted and corrupted** for non-traditional purposes. This is particularly so with people whose parents or grandparents migrated to towns and who no longer have any tangible connection to their original village and clan.

While it is a useful system in a subsistence economy it does not work well in the commercial environment. Among other things it imposes considerable **strains on working people**. This may involve having to share wages with unemployed *wantoks* and giving preference to unqualified and unsuitable *wantoks* when job opportunities arise.

This is particularly so in the public service and

is a major contributor to **inefficiency and mismanagement.** Many wage earners eventually decide that the effort is not worth it and abandon their jobs.

One of the other negative spinoffs of the *wantok* system is the extreme difficulty for individual entrepreneurs to successfully run **small businesses**. Many attempts fall prey to the unreasonable demands of relatives and clan members. Some wealthier Papua New Guinean business men have solved this problem by employing **expatriate managers** but for the average entrepreneur trying to establish a business this is not an option.

The *wantok* system can also work in a positive way for people wishing to start a business however. Small business loans are extremely difficult to obtain for Papua New Guineans because the banks and other lenders require collateral, such as land, as security for the loan. With land largely communally owned this is next to impossible. The only source of unsecured loans is through less creditable sources, such as loan sharks, who charge exorbitant interest rates.

Wantoks often contribute collectively to get a business off the ground. They seldom charge interest or set time limits for loan repayments and only expect to be repaid when the business starts to make money. This system has a domino effect where successful businessmen then help other *wantoks* to whom they are obligated to set up businesses of their own. Through this system highlanders have managed to monopolise bus and taxi services in the two largest cities of Port Moresby and Lae.

The nature of small scale passenger services in Papua New Guinea is such that it is not attractive to expatriate businessmen. Passenger Motor Vehicles (PMVs) venture out to isolated villages and taxis often ply their trade in squatter settlements which are considered unsafe. Such businesses also do not need large amounts of seed capital. In many cases they can begin with one truck or one car and build up from there.

Larger amounts of seed capital are required

when setting up businesses like trade stores. Also, with their arrays of tempting stock they tend to be targets of *wantoks*. Trade stores run by Papua New Guineans seldom seem to prosper for long. The void has been filled to a large extent by **Asian business men**.

The Chinese have been in Papua New Guinea for a long time and many of the families are highly respected but with the burgeoning resource developments there are many newcomers, some of whom are clearly **illegal immigrants** who have bribed their way into the country.

Small business is supposedly set aside by statute for the sole benefit of Papua New Guinean citizens but with the willingness of public servants at all levels to accept bribes there is no effective policing of the law. These newcomers who run the trade stores, fast food outlets, gambling, building services and minor engineering works are deeply resented by the average Papua New Guinean. Occasionally violence erupts and Asian stores and premises have been looted and torched. The recent practice of some resource developers to bring in **Asian labour** because it is more reliable and compliant has also added to this resentment and it is probably only a matter of time before it poses a security threat. To make matters worse, some of this labour brought in by the resource developers do not have the appropriate visas and are, in effect, also illegal immigrants.

Land is held communally by the clan. Individual clan members use the land by **mutual consent**.

Gardens tend to be moved to new areas on a regular basis as fertility drops off. When an area is depleted of good, easily accessible garden sites the village or hamlet is moved to a new area. In some areas this might happen every 10-20 years.

Some large villages, particularly on the coast and along the big rivers, have been in the same place for a long time however. A family or an individual 'owns' the garden that they cultivate while it is in use.

Abandoned gardens simply go back into the clan land pool. Individuals and families might also **own resources** on the land, such as economic trees, on an ongoing basis. It is reasonable to assume that every tree or economic resource on clan land is owned by someone.

Sometimes these resources, like sago stands or coconut trees, particularly if they have been deliberately planted, are passed on from father to son or mother to daughter.

The **communal** nature of land ownership has always made it difficult to develop land for commercial purposes in Papua New Guinea. Any area of land will have multiple owners with varying rights.

A clan member might be one of a number of primary owners but there are also secondary owners who might have a range of minor rights, such as the right to fish and hunt over the land, collect certain resources on the land or simply the right of egress to walk over it to get to somewhere else. **Primary and secondary land rights** can become extremely complex, particularly if there is a financial reward at stake.

The land and its resources are considered to be **inalienable.** Land is owned in a never ending continuum. No matter what happens to the land the original owners and their descendants consider the land to still be theirs.

This includes clans which have formally sold land to the government for lease to other users. The Motu/Koitabu people around Port Moresby, for instance, believe that the land on which the city lies still belongs to them. This even extends back to land lost to another clan through conquest.

Landowners also believe that they own any **minerals** under their land; they are resolute in this belief despite the assertion by the state that it owns all mineral and petroleum resources.

The problem of **multiple-ownership** is dealt with legally through the creation of **Indigenous Land Groups.** After registration these groups are legally constituted to deal with identified tracts of land on a commercial basis in the same way that individuals deal with land in western societies.

An ILG usually comprises the members of the clan claiming traditional ownership of the land. ILGs usually set up landowner companies to deal with **commercial matters**.

For Papua New Guineans traditional **agreements** between individuals and groups are open ended and are constantly coddled, modified and amended as circumstances change. This is in sharp contrast to western concepts of **contract**, which has set time limits and explicit delivery and output details set out in a legally immutable document.

Where an aberration in a western contract might be discounted or disregarded because it is beyond the scope of an original agreement in traditional society the aberration is simply taken on board, discussed and then added to the ongoing mix.

In traditional society a deal is not a deal but is merely an agreement to conduct an ongoing dialogue, exchange and negotiation about a matter.

Dispute resolution and negotiations in PNG tend to be dealt with as 'bundles' of problems rather than as single issues. There is no such thing as a quick resolution; disputes can go on for days, weeks, months and even years.

Sometimes it is difficult to pin down the actual problem. People circle issues and approach them from all sorts of angles. What might have seemed like the central issue may quickly dissipate and be replaced by another one and then another one after that. People build up to the central issue by working their way through minor issues first.

Disputes in western societies tend to be mediated in the **courts**. In many cases the litigants are relative strangers, as in, say, a tradesman and a disgruntled homeowner unhappy with the quality of work carried out. The aim is to extract **damages** that will compensate the aggrieved party for their loss or inconvenience. The court is primarily concerned with following the law and the emotional effects of its decision on the litigants are an irrelevant matter. Often litigants will leave the courtroom hating each other; the only consolation being that they will probably never meet again.

In Papua New Guinean dispute resolution the **aim is reconciliation and emotional closure**. Disputes taking place at the village or clan level are usually between people who know each other and will continue to live in close proximity. Most often the relatives of the people in dispute will involve themselves in the argument and become **part-owners of the problem**. Disputes need to be resolved in such a way that all of these people can pick up their lives without ongoing animosity hanging over them.

This is one reason why you might see compensation payments distributed in a much wider way than expected with relatives on both sides taking portions. The aim is for everyone to be happy with the outcome. This **egalitarian approach to the ownership of disputes** is often transferred to settlements between people in the clan and outside bodies like resource developers. In engaging in a dispute with a landowner say, the developer is more than likely to find itself engaging with his whole clan.

Pride and "face" is also extremely important in dispute resolution. People seldom admit guilt, particularly in public, and will never acknowledge breaches of tradition and custom.

Dispute resolution works best in **public forums** open to everyone. Going off to discuss issues privately simply creates suspicion. People taken aside in this way will also feel intimidated.

People in Papua New Guinea don't like making **decisions** on their own; they prefer to have others standing with them and agreeing with them. A person agreeing to something in private is likely to inexplicably change their mind in public and renege on an undertaking.

Offering people **incentives** in private is a sure way to escalate a problem beyond control. Taking someone aside for a heart-to-heart talk is also a very bad idea because people think that some sort of conspiracy is being hatched.

This reluctance to make and own decisions by individuals has ramifications for the management styles of Papua New Guinean people in leadership positions. **Avoiding making a decision** is a very fine art in Papua New Guinea.

Most people are reluctant to talk on behalf of others even though they might create this impression at the time. Only the 'right' people have authority to speak on particular issues. Establishing who the '**right' people** are is an important first step in any dispute resolution discussions.

Sometimes no one will know who the 'right' people are and establishing these credentials has to become part of the negotiation process. An eloquent and accomplished speaker in a meeting may not have any **authority** at all; the authority might lie with an individual hanging around in the background saying nothing.

Educated professionals in Papua New Guinea can hold their own anywhere in the world. There is, in fact, a 'brain-drain' occurring in the country. There are two main reasons for this. The first is the **higher rates of pay available overseas** and the second is the cultural inhibition in Papua New Guinea of being seen to rise up from the pack and **stand out in the crowd.** This second reason explains why some people who apparently have enormous potential often appear reluctant to strive to progress professionally.

Often a whole community or **clan will invest in a talented student** and help them get a higher education. This person then not only becomes a source of community pride but also becomes a community asset and a source of wealth, wisdom and leadership. Everyone in the clan follows the fortunes of such people and know exactly where they are working and for whom. A promotion or an award earned by such people is 'owned' and celebrated by the whole clan. Conversely, if the person fails in their work or gets dismissed the whole clan **feels the shame**. In contrast to those professionals who don't want to stand out in the crowd these people who are the objects of clan pride can be very aggressive and ambitious in their efforts to live up to expectations.

Living up to clan expectations can have detrimental effects on workers who are trying to live up to the collective pride associated with their job, particularly when *wantoks* take advantage of them. A worker who may have to support freeloading *wantoks* can be very tempted to borrow money. When they do this they usually go to unscrupulous **loan sharks**. A surprising number of workers in Papua New Guinea live from one pay packet to the next. Often they get weeks behind in paying off their loans and find themselves in debt to several loan sharks. Sometimes they might resort to gambling and the situation gets even worse. Losing their job can be disastrous. Cases of petty theft of business property can usually be traced to this source. Employees should be aware of these potential **debt loads** carried by their employees.

In both of these cases the ordinary assumptions that might be made in a western workplace don't fit. The intelligent but unassertive individual is so not because they lack ambition or drive and the aggressive individual may not necessarily be driven by personal ambition. In both cases the cultural context must be taken into account.

In many parts of Papua New Guinea, particularly the highlands, **theatricals** are part and parcel of the consensus process.

In many places **oratory** is a well-defined art and has formal and weighty **protocols**. Good orators are highly respected and it is an art that many successful expatriates in Papua New Guinea have mastered.

The ability to stand up in front of a crowd and present your case with appropriate dignity goes a long way during any negotiations. It is not something to be afraid of; shyness and fumbles with language are all taken in good humour and with grace. If an interpreter is used he or she will usually fix these up anyway. Unfortunately they might also add their own spin to what you've said so it's handy to have someone around who can pick this up.

An expatriate who can deliver a good speech in **Tok Pisin** goes a long way in Papua New Guinea.

Another form of theatrics involves **feigned emotion**, particularly **anger**. Some highlanders, for instance, are very good at this tactic and can rant and rave and look very threatening one minute and perfectly reasonable the next.

Everyone knows what is going on and they let it all run its course. No one would be silly enough to meet this feigned anger with anger in response. When that happens, the dynamics can change rapidly and result in **physical violence**.

It is important to be able to distinguish between feigned and real anger. Many Papua New Guineans can become angry and irrational very quickly. This is why it is never a good idea to stop and try to help people after a traffic accident, particularly if you are involved and people have been injured or killed. In highly emotional situations like this you will run a real risk of being injured or even killed if you stop. The best strategy is to drive immediately to the nearest police station. The police will provide protection for you and organise medical help for the injured.

There are other theatrics, some of them relatively new, like the reciting of prayers at the beginning and end of a meeting. These should be taken on board as part of the process of negotiation. If your hosts feel more comfortable observing these **formalities** it is wise to go along with them.

The outcomes of dispute resolution are **never cut and dried**. Dispute resolution is a **consensual process** which contrasts markedly with western concepts of **adversarial** encounters with clear **winners and losers**. They generally end with a set of **open-ended options** rather than an adjudicated decision.

Close questioning and **interrogation** or putting people on the spot or verbally working them into a corner is not a good idea. Going after an individual who seems to be at the heart of a problem is not a good idea, neither is isolating people.

Pride is at stake and for this reason in Papua New Guinean disputes there are seldom easily identifiable **winners and losers**. Reward and loss are much nuanced. Rather, people expect to come away from a dispute resolution with an outcome satisfactory to them.

Getting people to change from a previous position is fine as long as in the final outcome they are happy to do so – saving face is a paramount consideration. Identifying someone as a clear winner in a dispute is likely to result in increased antagonism which can be manifested in unexpected ways like **payback and revenge**.

Celebrating a successful dispute resolution with everyone involved, including winners and losers, is a traditional thing and seals any **bargains** struck. Failure to do this will weaken the seal. This can range from a handshake and a drink together to a formal event where speeches are made and gifts exchanged. It is well to humour this process.

While a bundle of issues may appear to have been settled there are usually other related issues left over for next time. For many dispute resolution is an enjoyable occupation and **something is always saved for later**. It is a matter of waiting for its time to come and it always pays to be alert to possibilities and attempts to push the packet as far as it will go.

Traditional society in Papua New Guinea is a **'throwaway' society**. If a house starts to fall down or a canoe starts to leak the natural thing to do is build a new one.

This attitude is reflected in peoples' attitudes to **infrastructure**. Rather than maintain what is already there people are more inclined to simply spend labour or money on a new one. Europeans find this very frustrating. They might build a school or an aid post in a community only to come back in a few years' time to find that it is falling down and that machinery like pumps and generators have ceased to operate.

In the workplace this is also common with **maintenance a low priority**. It takes acculturation to fix this problem, which takes time. This attitude is why otherwise viable infrastructure from before independence has fallen into disuse.

Europeans have a much more personal attachment to their 'stuff', especially prestige stuff like houses and cars and tend to look after them. When they look at them they see function but they also see dollars and cents.

Those whose **language** is both spoken and written tend to focus tightly on precise words for their communications: words whose meanings are largely fixed. Those whose language is purely **oral** use it in conjunction with all their other senses and in the context of their surroundings.

Their spoken and sung language has a constantly mutable nature, which exists only in the time it is breathed out. It is always **subject to context**, open to **change**. For traditional Papua New Guineans it is no use just understanding words: you have to know the precise context in which they are spoken.

For instance, suppose you are trying to ascertain the distance between two points which are separated by several steep valleys between which you intend to walk. The two points are visible to each other with the naked eye; therefore they are not very far apart at all.

However, to walk from one to the other will require several difficult descents, the crossing of swift flowing streams and ascents up very steep and difficult slopes. Should the day be wet these difficulties will be magnified.

When you ask whether is it very far between the two points your answer will come back loaded with context. The person supplying the answer will have considered the terrain, the likelihood of rain that week and a judgement about your skill as a walker. For them the walk might take a few hours but for you it might take many hours.

At the same time they will be considering the purpose for which you want to make the walk; if it is to deliver some good news or other largesse their response might be that the distance between the two places is short. If you plan to deliver some bad news their answer might be that it is a long way between the two points.

They will also be considering what sort of answer you might be expecting and be tailoring their response accordingly. Under these circumstances qualitative words like 'short', 'medium' and 'long' assume **different contextual meaning** and need to be teased out if any degree of exactitude is to be obtained.

Relationships are built up over time in PNG rather than formally imposed. Trust develops over time as people become more and more acquainted. This is in contrast to western societies where relationships beyond the circle of family and friends are often established because of the positions that people occupy.

In most new encounters between people in western societies the question of **occupation** is an early marker that needs to be established. What do you do for a living is a question which is inevitably asked early in the exploration of a new relationship?

In this sense the actual position that someone

occupies is more important than the individual. The reverse can be true in PNG. **Status and authority** must be earned rather than imposed.

Familiarity is very important to Papua New Guineans. One effect of the emphasis on developed rather than imposed relationships is an **aversion to change**. People are much happier to deal with people they trust and have known for some time.

To many people an individual's status in an exalted position is a secondary consideration or is an integrally entwined element together with their personality and individual attributes.

This can make it difficult for a new manager coming into a position where time does not allow long-term relationships to develop. The **constant change** in personnel in the commercial environment is extremely difficult for many people to handle. Someone who flies in for a meeting and then flies out again never to be seen again has little currency in Papua New Guinea. Just because you are the general manager of a company doesn't mean that you automatically deserve respect; that still has to be earned.

There is a widespread perception among ordinary Papua New Guineans that resource developers are causing widespread environmental damage and ignoring the social and economic needs of local people. It is also believed that successive Papua New Guinean governments have been intimidated by the larger companies and have been kowtowing to their demands by bending rules to accommodate them. There is also a widespread perception that the government lacks the skills required to negotiate equitable conditions for landowners. People believe that projects are planned overseas and that bottom up planning involving landowners is urgently required. They believe that compensation and capacity building in local communities should be a mandatory part of any resource development project. Communities need to feel involved and be part of a resource development program in their area and to derive a level of benefit from it.

While there have been a number of resource

developments in Papua New Guinea with considerable royalties paid to both the national and provincial governments the delivery of benefits to ordinary people in the form of **improved services**, such as health and education, and infrastructure, such as roads and bridges, has been extremely inefficient. With no visible benefits from such developments many ordinary people have concluded that the resource companies are only interested in exploiting Papua New Guinea for its wealth. A resource company may rightfully protest that it has paid royalties to the government and it is the government's fault rather than the fault of the company that benefits have not got back to the community but people still maintain that they have received no benefits from the company or the development.

Also, while Australia pours much aid into Papua New Guinea very little of it, except where it is specifically targeted, seems to reach the grassroots level. A lot of aid money is paid to expensive consultants for what seems to be an endless stream of studies and reports, even when the solution to the problem at hand is obvious. Aid is also often re-directed by the agencies to Australian consultants and contractors. This is referred to as 'boomerang' aid and the perception is that it is designed to enrich the consulting agencies rather than solving problems in Papua New Guinea. Untied aid funds are also siphoned off by unscrupulous and corrupt public servants and politicians.

Papua New Guinea is also an ideal 'playing field' for a multitude of research, particularly in the fields of anthropology and sociology. The results of this type of research seldom filter back down to the people who have been studied. The assumption is that once a researcher has got what they want out of a community, either for publication or to further their career, they will abandon the community. And the nature of many research projects is such that this often happens. Only a handful of researchers maintain ongoing relationships with the community that they study.

These sorts of perceptions of **exploitation by**

expatriates and the organisations and companies that they work for is widely held in Papua New Guinea. The model also fits in well with courses taught in colleges and universities, both in Papua New Guinea and overseas, in relation to colonial and post-colonial history. Under this model exploitation carried out by administrators in colonial times has been continued by multinational companies in post-colonial times. In this sense, expatriates in Papua New Guinea are often presumed by local people to be there solely to get something out of the country and its people.

This sense of suspicion is often reinforced by the actions of companies which are exclusively commercially driven and which refuse to become engaged in any form of local level philanthropic activity. When an expatriate is first introduced to a local Papua New Guinean community many in that community look first to establish and understand motives before they are prepared to talk or negotiate. Explaining one's motives as early as possible, even if they are entirely commercially driven, is always a good move.

Most resource developers in Papua New Guinea employ **community affairs** people. They are the link between the corporation and the local people. Some of the larger companies have set up community affairs departments in their local organisations.

These departments are sometimes staffed by professionals like anthropologists but more generally by people with long experience in Papua New Guinea. Patrol officers or kiaps, both European and local, from the colonial period are a significant component in these departments, although age is catching up with many of them and they are being replaced by people with a more disparate background.

In the modern age of profit driven business the advice of the community affairs officers tends to be given a low priority even though in the long run such advice can save costly delays, misunderstandings and unrest.

Some of the larger departments can take on a life of their own and they can become a law unto themselves. This is very noticeable when the departments take on a hard line attitude in their dealings with local people.

Because of their size the functions of the larger departments and their interactions with local people like landowners tends to take place with nominated representatives in board rooms rather that at the village level.

Taking clan leaders out of their environment and feting them in this way leads them to lose the trust of their community. Often clan leaders involved in such meetings fail to communicate decisions to the villagers. This leads to alternative leaders emerging in the villages and the perpetuation of the original issue.

A company may therefore incorrectly assume that a problem or issue has been resolved when in fact it has simply shifted to a new set of players. Even if a group of landowners arrive at the company headquarters in Port Moresby for negotiations it is highly probable that they have personal agendas which they wish to hide from scrutiny.

It is always best to conduct landowner

negotiations on site so that everyone can see what is going on.

There is also a strong case for using outside community affairs experts who are seen to have a level of neutrality and no vested interests in either the company or with the landowners.

The **treatment of women** in Papua New Guinea is a vexed question, just as it is in many western industrial societies. It has been said that in the traditional setting men's priorities are in the order of land first, pigs next and women last.

There are, however, striking similarities between the position of women in Papua New Guinea and those in so-called more sophisticated societies. In both, for instance, women are regarded by many men not only as **second class citizens** but as **chattels and commodities**.

For some men in western societies the role of women is clearly defined as being purely supportive of their men. The employers of many men still accept that a wife's role is to provide unpaid labour and other needs, like producing more children who will become workers, so that the man can engage unencumbered in paid work. The employer is, in effect, getting two people for the price of one. This was the situation at the end of the Industrial Revolution and it is still largely the situation today.

In traditional society in Papua New Guinea the woman's role is to tend the gardens, look after the pigs, cook the food and produce fine sons to carry on the clan line. A man may take several wives to increase his capacity to keep more pigs and expand his gardens. More pigs and more produce for distribution in the traditional exchange network will increase his power and prestige in the clan. Even many highly educated women knowingly and willingly engage in **polygamy**. Custom is not something that disappears with education.

The treatment of women as chattels is slowly changing in both societies as **education** levels increase but violence against women is still a problem. In western societies this violence is more likely to take a **psychological** form while in Papua New Guinea it is chiefly manifested in overt violence.

An expatriate who may have subjected his wife to debilitating psychological stress and trauma will, nevertheless, still be appalled by the violence perpetuated against women in Papua New Guinea.

Despite many gains by women for **equality** in both societies there is still a long way to go. A pot calling a kettle black is no solution.

In a society living close to the earth the reality that life can be "nasty, brutish and short" is very much in evidence. Cycles of plenty and paucity, depending upon the weather, has also always been a reality in the traditional setting.

This rawness of existence is often demonstrated in the way people treat each other as well as the way in which they treat their animals. Casual cruelty, such as deliberately blinding or crippling domestic pigs so that they don't wander and keeping hunting dogs at near starvation levels so that they are more eager to hunt, are inherent cruelties which people have become inured to.

Most expatriates in their own country, unless they are farmers, are divorced from the way their food is produced. When they go into a supermarket to buy a pork chop for dinner they seldom consciously make the connection between the chop and a once live pig. For many expatriates their **relationship to animals** is formed through having a pet dog or cat which they feed regularly from tins of specially made pet food. For these people their attitude to animals is often shaped by their relationship to a well fed pet cat or dog and when they come to Papua New Guinea they are ill prepared to see life in the raw.

The treatment of animals in traditional societies is often a contributing factor to the culture shock mentioned earlier. Many expatriates will exhibit a degree of discomfort and distaste when they enter a village situation and see underfed dogs and things like pigs that have been blinded or crippled to stop them wandering and getting into gardens. It is a reaction similar to the sadness that some village women feel when their favourite pig is taken away to be killed for a *singsing*.

Slipping a skinny dog in a village your lunchtime ham sandwich might make you feel better but it won't solve the problem of cruelty; the dog will still be hungry the next day after you leave and your sandwich might be the difference between a hunter catching a bush pig or losing it. Alternatively, a thin dog in a village may not necessarily be starved; it may simply be an extremely fit hunting dog. Many hunters value their dogs highly and take good care of them. Rather than starving them they feed them special potions, leaves and food to enhance their prowess.

From the Papua New Guinean Perspective

Prior to about 1740 society and culture in Europe and America was in many ways like society and culture in Papua New Guinea. People lived in villages or small towns and grew their own food and seldom ventured far from home. Children, parents and grandparents all lived close to each other.

In some places, like Ireland and Scotland, several villages formed part of a larger clan and could trace their origins to a common ancestor. These clans had chiefs. In other areas, like England, feudal lords, who had inherited their status and wealth, were leaders and assumed a kind of exploitive responsibility for the people in the villages.

This period is sometimes referred to as 'pre-industrial'. Traditional society in Papua New Guinea is also sometimes called pre-industrial.

From about 1740 in Europe and America there were **rapid developments in technology** which led to the invention of labour saving machines and a basic change in the way commodities were manufactured.

This development is now referred to as the **Industrial Revolution** and it caused major changes in the way western society was organised. It was also the coming of age of a system called **capitalism**. Capitalism spread rapidly and is now the basis on which many societies in the world are organised.

One of the key things that capitalism changed was how wealth was created and distributed and how people related to each other. These changes are important in understanding the differences between expatriates and most of the people in Papua New Guinea.

At a very basic level when expatriates and rural people in Papua New Guinea interact it is a **meeting of two very different societies**; an industrial society and a pre-industrial society. On this basis it is inevitable that there will be difficulties in understanding.

In their home countries expatriates live in a society divided by **class;** upper class, middle class and lower or working class. Sometimes countries like Australia and America claim to be classless societies but when they are subject to close analysis this proves to be untrue.

In earlier times one's position in the hierarchy of class was firmly fixed from birth and ordinary people had little hope of moving into a higher class. In those times the lucky individuals who were born into the upper classes inherited the wealth that resided there.

Nowadays the transition upward through the classes is much easier and more fluid. This has created a situation where the boundaries of class are nowhere near as rigid. People can now aspire to become 'upwardly mobile' and it is common for people from poor backgrounds to acquire wealth, power and prestige through diligence and ability rather than privilege.

However, while there is now more class mobility, an individual's place in a particular class is still a reality.

A person's membership of a particular class is primarily defined by **personal wealth**; how much money they have in the bank, how big their house is and what sort of car they own.

To a lesser degree a person's **level of education** influences which class they belong to. At the top are the very wealthy and/or highly educated and at the bottom are the very poor and uneducated.

When an expatriate sees a person in a village with a small house, few possessions and the inability to read and write they can unconsciously feel **superior** and regard that person as lower class and inferior. This attitude can wash off onto Papua New Guineans and can make them feel inferior to expatriates. In reality, neither person is superior or inferior to the other.

In expatriate society people at the bottom aspire to move up through the classes to the top while those already up there guard their position jealously.

This idea of class produces a society which is ordered in a **hierarchy**, like the top and bottom of a social ladder. Hierarchy is reflected in all aspects of expatriate life. Companies are ordered in hierarchies with the bosses at the top and the ordinary workers, like labourers, at the bottom.

The bosses also guard their positions **jealously** and live in fear of being replaced. A person's place in this system of hierarchy is very important because it defines their level of success and informs their **self-worth**.

The existence of a strict hierarchy in the organisation of a society makes its members very **competitive**. In striving to work their way up through the hierarchy they have to compete with other people doing the same thing.

This competitive attitude **isolates** people at the personal level and makes them suspicious of each other and they tend to act as **individuals** rather than as a group. 'Looking after number one' is a key characteristic of a capitalist society and the 'rights of the individual' are extolled and placed ahead of the rights of the general population or 'the common good'.

Individualism creates a **desire to win** and this is reflected in all aspects of expatriate life. While the acquisition of wealth is a driving force the desire to win is equally as strong. The wealthy upper class are regarded as '**winners**' while the poor working class are regarded as '**losers**'.

To demonstrate one's ambition and capabilities it is necessary to adopt the persona of a winner. So when at expatriate plays sport, for instance, they do so not just for simple enjoyment but to demonstrate their prowess as a winner. This is one reason why successful sports people in Australia are paid lots of money and why Australia strives so hard at the Olympic Games to win gold medals.

Looking after number one means that people need to be **independent**. They cannot afford to have a lot of relatives who need support hanging around and dipping into the wealth that they are accumulating. For this reason they live in **nuclear families** and limit the number of children they have.

A typical nuclear family consists of a man, his wife, two or three children and a dog or cat. Sometimes there might be an elderly parent living in the house but when age catches up with a couple they usually move into a retirement home and then a nursing home.

For an expatriate one of the reasons for spending a lifetime **accumulating wealth** is so that they can live in comfort in their old age. Unlike Papua New Guinea old people do not expect their children to look after them when they become frail. They will tell you that they do not wish to impose that sort of **burden** on their children.

In most cases adult children and their elderly parents and uncles and aunts live apart, often some distance away in other towns and states. Gatherings of relatives only occur on special occasions such as weddings and funerals.

These events are conducted with a sense of necessary reluctance and everyone breathes a sigh of relief when they are over and they can go home.

Individualism and nuclear families are also encouraged within capitalist society because they increase the number of people to whom goods can be sold. **Selling and consuming material goods** is a major preoccupation in expatriate society. One reason why this is so is that their wealth has made their lives very comfortable and buying things provides a kind of satisfaction.

Generally this satisfaction is short lived and people feel the need to go out and buy more things. Even in poor areas people's houses are overflowing with goods that they have bought and no longer use. All this buying and selling is a major driving factor in western economies and is encouraged by their governments. Everywhere you go in western countries you will see messages and advertisements exhorting you to buy, buy and keep buying.

In a village situation, where electricity and

reception are available, there might be one television set in one house and everyone comes around to watch it on special occasions like football finals. In the village there is no reason for every house to have a television set because it is a shared resource. In a western suburb each house and apartment will have its own television set along with its own refrigerator, washing machine, electric stove, toaster and other commodities and to suggest that people **share** them would be viewed with dismay. An expatriate might lend his neighbour a shovel but he would never lend him his television set.

Expatriates are also wary about sharing their time and they make a definite distinction between **working time and leisure time**. Because they work so they can buy everything they need rather than growing or hunting or making it themselves they place a definite value on their time.

'Time is money' is a common expression and because of the value that time has it is jealously guarded as if it were a commodity. This is why expatriates strictly separate their work and private lives.

An expatriate preoccupation in relation to time is often referred to in relation to their **quality of life.** Expatriates will also talk about time in terms of life style balance and will complain about working hard and earning lots of money but having little time to spend with their wives and children. They call this being **money rich and time poor**. For this reason you will find that many expatriates will avoid **mixing** with their fellow workers outside the workplace.

Because time is equated with money expatriates are also very conscious about **managing time** and making the best use of it. Spending time wisely is equated with spending money wisely. It is a valuable commodity and should not be wasted or frittered away on frivolous things.

This is why they get frustrated when Papua New Guineans take a leisurely approach to getting things done and insist upon letting everyone have their say in meetings, especially when they each repeat the same thing. To an expatriate this is **wasting time** and since time is valuable it is also wasting money.

Because the acquisition of wealth and the accumulation of status bearing commodities is a driving force in capitalist society the competition for the best jobs which pay the highest wages is intense.

At one time it was possible for people with drive and ambition to make money by working hard and being shrewd and crafty but the number of 'self-made' people has decreased in recent years and the emphasis has shifted to **education**.

In most industries and professions now the people who rise to the top are the well-educated. In general society parading one's possessions is considered vulgar but parading one's **qualifications** is normal and expected.

This trend away from self-taught skills and experience towards education and appropriate qualifications has created a dramatic shift in the way education is delivered. Years ago the main motivation for attending school and university was to learn and gain knowledge but nowadays this motivation has become secondary to acquiring qualifications to get a job.

On the job training such as through apprenticeships has been declining for many years. As a result education, particularly at universities, has acquired the same status as material commodities in capitalist society and has to be bought and paid for. Instead of being places of learning and knowledge universities have become industries churning out graduates as if they were products.

This trend means that expatriates **value formal qualifications highly**. This is applicable across a whole range of jobs ranging from someone like a geologist with a good degree to a fork lift operator with the appropriate licence and training.

For Papua New Guineans who have acquired a skill by learning on the job over the years this presents a problem when they haven't got an appropriate certificate. An expatriate will tend to judge you by whatever certificates you hold, not by your ability to do the job.

As everyone is aware there is now a tendency for some people to counterfeit or buy counterfeit or fake certificates. The big companies are aware of this because it is something that happens in capitalist society too and they scrutinise people's qualifications very closely.

The need to do this is twofold. Firstly, they want to get properly skilled people in their organisation or company. Secondly, if someone has an accident at work because they didn't have the appropriate qualifications and skills the insurance that the company holds will not pay for medical treatment or replacement of damaged machinery.

Because expatriates coming to Papua New Guinea are usually well-educated they tend to deal with issues on a **rational or scientific** basis. Even though many of them are Christians, especially the Americans, they do not generally believe in things like miracles or divine intervention.

They are also highly sceptical about sorcery and magic. They believe that everything that happens has a **logical cause** which can be explained in scientific terms. This might range from an unexplained illness or death suffered by a worker to something like a landslip or flood.

For many Papua New Guineans the activities of a mining company or other developer in an area can cause unexplained things to happen. If a pipeline or road disturbs a sacred site, which is the home of a significant ancestor, subsequent events like flooding and landslips will be interpreted as the ancestor seeking revenge by Papua New Guineans but for an expatriate they will just be **natural events**.

Instead of being the work of an aggrieved ancestor or spirit the events are seen as the result of a low pressure system out at sea causing heavy inland rain over an area which is geologically unstable and prone to erosion. Claims from local people for **compensation** are therefore viewed as unjustified or as opportunistic grabs for money, even though the local people firmly believe that the actions of the company caused the catastrophe.

The fault here is not so much that the beliefs of the local people are unscientific or illogical but more because the expatriates are unaware of the possibilities of local beliefs and customs. An expatriate in charge of a work gang might sack an older man who is not working well without realising that he is a clan leader who is highly respected by the other men. When the men go on strike and refuse to work until the old man is given his job back the expatriate becomes puzzled and can't work out what's going on.

He knows that the old man is not as strong as his fellows and cannot keep up with them and sacking him and replacing him with a younger man is **logical.** He is unaware of the damage done to the old clan leader's pride in being replaced by a *manki nating* and of the precedent he has created by ignoring an important aspect of custom.

His attitude might also be that 'we're not in the village now and we do things my way, not your way'. He may not entirely believe this and he may be sympathetic to the old man but he will have a boss of his own looking over his shoulder demanding that work progress efficiently. If it doesn't his own job might be on the line.

In the case of the damage to the sacred ancestor's home and the sacking of the respected elder and leader the only way to avoid such situations is to make the expatriates aware of them as issues as soon as possible.

Many Papua New Guineans, particularly those who have been exposed to western ways and education, find it embarrassing to explain these sorts of beliefs and customs and are often reluctant to do so because they think the expatriate will think that they believe in the same things but in the long run doing so can avoid misunderstanding and its consequences.

A good way to alert an expatriate boss is to do it through someone like a community affairs officer. A good community affairs officer will pass the information on and will be able to explain it to the expatriate boss, even if they are sceptical about it themselves.

Just like everything else in capitalist society **land** is regarded as a **commodity** with a **fixed value** which can be **bought and sold**.

In Australia and America land is **owned privately** by individuals, sometimes jointly, or by corporations. Other land is held by the government. Land held privately by individuals and corporations is either held under a title called freehold or through long term lease.

Although some land, particularly farms in rural areas, may remain in a family through many generations and is passed on through sons and daughters there is generally **no great emotional attachment** to it.

Whereas a person in Papua New Guinea might have strong ties to their clan land in countries like Australia and America this sentiment is directed more widely to the country itself and is expressed in the notion of **nationhood.** Americans tend to be extremely patriotic in this respect but Australians are catching up. The feelings that a Papua New Guinean might have in relation to their clan land is very similar to the feelings that an expatriate has for his or her country.

The differences in the way that Papua New Guineans and expatriates regard land and the way that they deal with it can create a lot of problems. While an expatriate can vaguely appreciate a Papua New Guinean's view of land they see it as a great **drawback** rather than as a positive strength.

This is particularly so when it comes to developing land for **commercial purposes**. In this sense they regard traditional land tenure in Papua New Guinea as intrinsically problematic. Rather than seeing the system as nurturing the clan and providing its livelihood expatriates see it more as an **impediment to progress**.

Because expatriates live in a class-based and hierarchical society the position of an individual is very important. As such the **people who make decisions are the leaders and bosses**. While lip service is occasionally paid to the idea of consensus in reality it is the people in charge who make all the decisions.

A manager might invite comments from his staff over an issue and take their opinions into account but he always retains the ultimate veto and is responsible for the outcome. Managers in modern companies are encouraged to involve their staff in decision making but this is often done in a cynical way and the manager has either already made up his mind about an issue or has no intention of following any staff advice.

Managers with this **autocratic approach** are hard to pick and it is best to humour a manager even if you know he will ignore what you say.

Because their managers and bosses are the people who make decisions some expatriates are **reluctant to make decisions** about an issue independently. They do this because they lack authority, partly because the organisation has a set of expected norms which are part of the organisations workplace culture. They know that any decision they might make can be reversed by their boss. They also know that if they make the wrong decision they will be held personally responsible for it.

When you ask an expatriate for something, or to decide about a particular matter and they defer their response until later it is usually because they want to check with their boss first. They won't admit this because it reflects on their status in the company. So if you ask to speak to their boss about the matter so you can get an answer they are likely to react negatively and feel affronted.

Sometimes a question will have to travel up the line of command and through the hands of many people until one of them thinks he has the necessary authority to provide an answer.

Your original question may be misinterpreted and misunderstood by the time it reaches this decision maker. Of course, some expatriates will defer giving an answer by sending a question up the line even if they have the authority to deal with it as a way of either **avoiding the issue** or as a way of delaying it in the hope that you will forget about it.

In Papua New Guinean society such an issue will never die but in expatriate society many issues are consigned to the graveyard of unanswered problems, this is a widely accepted practice and known as 'none decision making' which exists in many large western organisations. Papua New Guineans will find this approach to issues just as frustrating as expatriates find Papua New Guineans insisting on a clan consensus before they are prepared to personally agree to anything.

In any society there are family and peer group pressures on individuals that largely dictate how they behave. When an individual moves into an environment where these pressures don't exist their behaviour can change, sometimes in subtle ways but often in unexpected ways. In some cases these changes are good; people under stress can become more relaxed and adjust their lifestyles to the slower pace of Papua New Guinean life. In other cases the changes are not so good.

Without these constraining pressures people tend to take risks that they wouldn't normally contemplate in their own society. These risks may include such things as excessive socialising and drinking, promiscuity and aggression. At a deeper level this sort of changed behaviour may point to **normally repressed psychological undercurrents** which they now feel free to unleash.

Something like this happens to Papua New Guineans when they move from a village environment into an urban setting. Expatriates in Papua New Guinea, especially those on short term contracts, are also prone to such change. In a colloquial sense they 'play up'.

In the commercial setting, when individuals are removed from the direct supervision of their bosses and often find themselves in positions of authority that they have not enjoyed before, their reactions can be quite marked. Their behaviour may range from simply taking **extra-long lunch breaks** to exercising **harsh, arrogant and overbearing behaviour** towards their subordinates and the other people, like members of the public, with whom they deal and interact.

This sort of behaviour is just as annoying to other expatriates who have a long term personal commitment to Papua New Guinea as it is to Papua New Guineans who have to work with them.

These people are essentially making their own rules of behaviour. However, in doing so they are often flouting the normative ideals with which they have been brought up. Expatriates, by and large, come from strictly law-abiding societies, and such behaviour is not normal but aberrant.

Societies in Australia and America are very large compared to those in Papua New Guinea. Many American cities have populations numbered in several millions. Because their society is ordered in a hierarchical way and because individualism is highly prized it is necessary to have **strong laws** which are rigidly enforced to maintain order and to ensure that society operates efficiently.

In Papua New Guinea where most people live in clans in rural areas social control is exercised through such things as shame and the fear of retribution or revenge. These sorts of controls do not really exist in capitalist society and it is necessary to have very specific laws to ensure order and to make sure everything operates as it should. Expatriates appreciate the need for these laws and have a **great respect** for them.

Laws cover all aspects of life in a capitalist society, including civil matters such as the way business is done. One of the most important aspects in relation to civil law is the concept of the **contract**.

A contract is an **agreement** between two or more individuals or corporate bodies about the way they will deal with each other. Most contracts are spelled out in fine detail and recorded in a **formal document**. On the other hand a contract can be as simple as a verbal agreement sealed with a handshake.

In either case, the details of the agreement are discussed in detail and completely understood before a contract is sealed. When one party breaches the contract or does something outside what has been agreed the aggrieved party expects to have recourse to the law and largely relies on **the courts** to rule on any compensation or other arrangement to satisfy the wrong done to them.

This is why contracts are so important to expatriates and why they insist upon having them formally set out on paper and agreed to with the signatures of all concerned. This is especially so when they are dealing with people that they don't know that well or when they are dealing with people they don't fully understand or trust. Traditional landowners generally fall into this latter category.

With a written contract they know they have recourse to the law if things go wrong. If a matter is not detailed in a contract, written or otherwise, expatriates are reluctant to entertain it.

If, for instance, a company agrees to supply a vehicle for the use of a landowner group and the landowners come looking for fuel to run it they are likely to be met with the response that the provision of fuel and maintenance is not in the contract and cannot therefore be supplied.

If something comes up that sounds like a good idea but isn't in the contract it is dealt with by formally amending the contract. All of these reasons mean that when you are negotiating a contract with a company it is a good idea to **include as much detail as possible**.

Contracts can cover all sorts of situations. When a man takes on a **job with a company**, even if it is for a short time he is entering into a contract. The contract will specify who he is and what he is to do and the fact that he has agreed to supply his labour at a specified rate of pay for a specified period of time.

Failing to turn up for work without a good reason is a breach of that contract and provides a legal reason to sack the man. Not obeying reasonable requests or performing a task below the required level are other reasons which can lead to someone being sacked for **breach of their contract.**

At the same time if a worker is asked to do something unreasonable, like constantly working over and above the time agreed he will have good reason to complain because the employer or company as the other party to the agreement has also breached the contract.

Because time is money and because work has a

monetary value expatriates have a strong **work ethic**. This is sometimes referred to as the Protestant Work Ethic because Protestantism was the main religion of the capitalists responsible for the Industrial Revolution.

Whereas a Papua New Guinean might grow weary or bored with doing a job and go off for a nap or go fishing or start to muck around on the job an expatriate is more likely to keep at it until either knock off time arrives or the job is complete.

Sometimes expatriates become quite obsessed about getting a job done and will work extra hours without pay to do it. This is particularly so when a project is running behind schedule. Many expatriates derive great satisfaction in this respect and they tend to expect their Papua New Guinean workers to be the same.

For an expatriate their **job adds meaning to their existence** and is part of their **personal identity** and they don't realise that for many Papua New Guineans work is part of a more diverse range of things, such as their life in the clan, which gives the meaning to their lives.

Expatriates who don't have a strict work ethic tend to be regarded as lazy or too laid back. Following a strict work ethic tends to be very stressful, although people sometimes don't realise they are stressed or will deny it. In any event **stress** of this nature can lead to short tempers and anger which some expatriates have difficulty in controlling.

Stress can be very dangerous to health and when combined with things like alcohol, drugs and tobacco can lead to major health problems and even death. Stressed expatriates can usually be spotted from their physical appearance and behaviour but this is not always the case. It pays to be wary of these people until you get to know them better.

Most expatriates live in the present. They are mostly concerned about what is happening today and in the future. **Planning ahead** is a big feature in expatriate life and many of them know exactly what they are going to be doing years ahead of time.

They tend to give the past, including history and tradition little thought. This is also true because their attachments to particular places are not strong.

It is also a trend which you will see among Papua New Guineans who have lived in the towns and cities for several generations. When the link to the clan is weakened tradition becomes less important and sometimes even irrelevant.

This is not so much the case with people who live in rural areas. To them many of their traditions and customs still dictate the way they live their lives and determines who can do what and where.

Most expatriates will listen politely to an elder explaining a tradition or custom but their interest quickly wanes. If there is a dispute about ownership of land which a company wants to use then their interest will increase but what they are really looking for is a ruling about the matter rather than all the details.

A few expatriates find tradition and custom very interesting and will listen closely and may even want to record information by writing it down or photographing places and things. These people generally have no ulterior motives and simply enjoy learning about other cultures.

Exchanging stories about one's history and culture, whether it is an expatriate or a Papua New Guinean, can be a great way to break the ice and begin building up relationships and trust.

A company which goes out of its way to learn about the area in which it is working and shows respect for local customs and traditions generally turns out to be a better company than one which ignores and has no patience for such matters.

Unlike Papua New Guineans who take pride in the formalities of meetings and negotiations, including the theatrics, the oratory and the displays of emotion that accompany them, expatriates tend to adopt a much more **reserved approach**. In their highly competitive society the outward **display of emotions** is seen as a **weakness** rather than a strength and commitment.

Worse still, they think emotions can be a mirror of what you are thinking and giving away such information can place you at a distinct disadvantage. For this reason expatriates tend to present a '**poker face**' during meetings and negotiations.

A poker face is a card gambling term where you keep a completely bland and expressionless look on your face so as not to give away what sort of cards you have in your hand. Some executives have even been known to have Botox injections to paralyse the nerves in their faces so that they don't inadvertently give the game away by frowning or smiling.

Many Papua New Guineans find this method of negotiating very disconcerting and interpret it as disinterest, indifference and coldness. In some cases this is exactly right but in most cases it is an **adopted mannerism** and **tactic** which they will drop once they become more familiar with how things work in Papua New Guinea.

When an expatriate gives someone a **gift** or do something to help them they don't generally expect anything in return. Neither does it involve creating an **obligation** on the part of the person receiving the gift. In most cases they simply enjoy being able to do so.

Sometimes gifts are given to validate a new friendship or to reinforce an old one. Gifts are most often given by expatriates to relatives and friends. At other times the gift may be a demonstration of their power and wealth. The fact that nothing is expected back except some sort of admiration reinforces the potency of the gift.

Gifts need to be differentiated from **loans**. A loan generally involves money and does have an expectation that it will be paid back at some stage. Generally a loan will follow a direct request and the terms of its repayment will be made clear.

For the Papua New Guinean worker there is no real way to gain knowledge about the way expatriates think beyond actual engagement with them. This can be a daunting task and is fraught with risks of misinterpretation and intent. This is why it is incumbent upon expatriate workers to be aware that differences exist between you and them and to assist you wherever possible. As noted elsewhere, the impressions you might have about expatriates, if they are gleaned from popular media such as television and movies, and even books can be quite misleading. Most expatriates don't act like film stars, they are usually just ordinary people like you who have been brought up in a different cultural environment with different beliefs and different ways of doing things. To many Papua New Guineans expatriates might seem mentally smart but physically clumsy – why do they keep tripping over tree roots in the forest, why can't they see them and step over them? The answer is because they are in an environment that is new and strange. Just as they need to be patient in their relationship with you, you need to be patient with them.

Gaining and Using Cultural Knowledge

For the expatriate the situation surrounding engagement with Papua New Guineans must be a well-planned and an ongoing process throughout the life of any project. Crucial to this are the attitudes of the workers on the frontline. A simple misstep by even the most junior worker can queer a project right from the start and result in unnecessary delays and financial losses. **The lack of cultural awareness among company employees is a significant factor in the breakdown of relations with landholders.** The only way to overcome this possibility is to ensure that all workers have an appreciation and knowledge of the cultural situation into which they are venturing. The easiest way to make this happen is to carry out a preliminary **social mapping** study.

The underlying principles of social mapping are based on a notion defined in Papua New Guinea's Constitution under the heading *National Goals of Papua New Guinea*, which recognises the value of traditional ways of life and culture, especially land ownership, and attempts to creatively include them in the process of economic and social development. Social mapping seeks to develop an understanding of the cultural and historical factors that have shaped both the traditional and contemporary relationship between the people and their land.

Social mapping in Papua New Guinea is used across a wide range of industries and government departments. In some cases, and at different levels, it is a mandatory requirement. In other cases it is simply used as a **convenient and effective planning tool**. It is also a concept that is generally understood in most parts of the country. A preliminary social mapping study is not an expensive exercise. Most studies can be carried out as desktop exercises combined with one or two **short field trips**. In most cases a short field trip will reveal whether traditional societies are holding up or whether they have undergone social change or even broken down. A myriad of **data** is now available on the internet and primary research is seldom required. There are very few areas in Papua New Guinea where cultural and social data are not already available. Not least are the colonial period patrol reports which contain very useful information and, quite often, very detailed area studies. Social mapping studies should be broad ranging with a **multidisciplinary** bias. Apart from issues related to culture and land the study can also consider logistical matters, including available infrastructure and its condition. Any such study should be written in plain English so that it is intelligible to ordinary workers, local people and landowners.

The logic of providing a copy of the preliminary social mapping study to a community is to demonstrate that you are genuinely concerned about them and any issues they might have. Most importantly, it will also demonstrate that you want to have an understanding of them and their customs. Studies with lots of old and new photographs are particularly well received. You should also be prepared to accept corrections and advice from the community about the report. Sometimes early anthropological research is flawed and/or particular customs are no longer followed. As a project proceeds additional data can be added to the report. This can be done by on-ground community liaison officers. It is a good idea to use Papua New Guinean community liaison officers wherever possible. The whole process is relatively simple and relies on good preparatory groundwork, good communications, good public relations skills, diligent data collection, effective reporting and, above all, patience.

Summary

I'll make this short because what all of the above boils down to, for both expatriates and Papua New Guineans, are the simple propositions of reflection and communication.

If you stop and think about what you are doing, or have done, and allow yourself to think a little bit outside the square it is remarkable how better things can work out. By simply asking yourself how you could have done something better can reap amazing dividends.

And when you are doing that don't be afraid to seek advice. Ask your Papua New Guinean offsiders what they think might be the best way to handle a situation. And when an expatriate asks you for advice don't tell him what he wants to hear. Tell it like it is.

And when things don't work out, don't just simmer in the background, make your position known to your co-workers and superiors. In other words, communicate, communicate across your cultures. It works, you've just got to try it. You might even discover that you are not all that different after all.

ABOUT THE AUTHOR

Philip Fitzpatrick studied Anthropology and Law at the Australian School of Pacific Administration and has degrees in Literature and Government from the University of Queensland. He is an Associate Member of the Australian Institute of Aboriginal and Torres Strait Islander Studies and a member of the Anthropological Society of South Australia. He was a field officer in Papua New Guinea between 1967 and 1973. Between 1974 and 1994 he was successively a Site Recorder, Registrar of Aboriginal Sites and Manager of the Aboriginal Heritage Branch in South Australia. Since 1994 he has worked as an independent consultant in both Australia and Papua New Guinea. To date, he has carried out over 300 heritage surveys and written numerous detailed social mapping, native title and heritage research reports. He also carries out pro bono work among indigenous communities in both Australia and Papua New Guinea. He is widely published, in both academic and popular media. He is the author of six novels. In 2010 he co-founded a national annual literature competition in Papua New Guinea. He also edits and publishes the annual Papua New Guinea Crocodile Literary Prize Anthology.